BETTER MARKS
In
LESS TIME
With
MORE FUN

Dave Blakemore and Dean Mathieson

ISBN 0 620 30838 9

Published by Reach Publishers, P.O.Box, 1384, Wandsbeck, South Africa, 3631
Printed and bound by Pinetown Printers (Pty) Ltd, 16 Ivy Road, Pinetown, 3600
Cover designed by Reach Publishers

Contents

A Successful Start

What to expect! Well, what we are going to do is to take you through a change of mindset in terms of how we approach studying and exams. For far too long people have looked at studying and exams in exactly the same way! It's time for a change...

What this book aims to show is that studying can be easy, creative and dare we say even fun.

All we ask you is that you just go with the flow. There are several exercises to help you build your ability in this way of studying and recalling information. Each exercise will not only help prove the point but also show you how easy it is to apply each of these techniques.

With a little bit of practice applying the techniques in the book, you will find that the amount of time you spend studying, will be less, while what you will recall actually increases.

All we ask is that you give it a chance, turn on your imagination and have some fun.

If you are ready, turn over to begin!

Testing Time!!!

Y ou have 5 minutes to remember the capitals of the 50 African countries listed below. Starting **NOW!!!**

After 5 minutes turn over and fill in your answers. You only have 5 minutes to record your answers.

Tick Tock!

Countries	Capitals	Countries	Capitals
ALGERIA	Algiers	LIBYA	Tripoli
ANGOLA	Luanda	MADAGASCAR	Antananarivo
BENIN	Porta Novo	MALAWI	Lilongwe
BOTSWANA	Gaborone	MALI	Bamako
BURKINA FASO	Ouagadougou	MAURITANIA	Nouakchott
BURUNDI	Bujumbura	MOROCCO	Rabat
CAMEROON	Yaounde	MOZAMBIQUE	Maputo
CAPE VERDE	Praia	NAMIBIA	Windhoek
CENTRAL AFRICAN REPUBLIC	Bangui	NIGER	Niamey
CHAD	N'djamena	NIGERIA	Lagos
COMOROS	Moroni	RWANDA	Kigali
CONGO	Brazzaville	SAO TOME AND PRINCIPE	Sao Tome
DJIBOUTI	Djibouti City	SENEGAL	Dakar
EGYPT	Cairo	SIERRA LEONE	Freetown
EQUATORIAL GUINEA	Malabo	SOMALIA	Mogadishu
ETHIOPIA	Addis Ababa	SOUTH AFRICA	Pretoria
GABON	Libreville	SUDAN	Khartoum
GAMBIA	Banjul	SWAZILAND	Mbabane
GHANA	Accra	TANZANIA	Dodoma
GUINEA	Conakry	TOGO	Lome
GUINEA-BISSAU	Bissau	TUNISIA	Tunis
IVORY COAST	Abidjan	UGANDA	Kampala
KENYA	Nairobi	ZAIRE	Kinshasa
LESOTHO	Maseru	ZAMBIA	Lusaka
LIBERIA	Monrovia	ZIMBABWE	Harare

Gong Gong Gong

Recording Your Answers

Remember only 5 Minutes!!!

Let's get ready to rumble!

Countries	Capitals	Countries	Capitals
ALGERIA		LIBYA	
ANGOLA		MADAGASCAR	
BENIN		MALAWI	
BOTSWANA		MALI	
BURKINA FASO		MAURITANIA	
BURUNDI		MOROCCO	
CAMEROON		MOZAMBIQUE	
CAPE VERDE		NAMIBIA	
CENTRAL AFRICAN REPUBLIC		NIGER	
CHAD		NIGERIA	
COMOROS		RWANDA	
CONGO		SAO TOME AND PRINCIPE	
DJIBOUTI		SENEGAL	
EGYPT		SIERRA LEONE	
EQUATORIAL GUINEA		SOMALIA	
ETHIOPIA		SOUTH AFRICA	
GABON		SUDAN	
GAMBIA		SWAZILAND	
GHANA		TANZANIA	
GUINEA		TOGO	
GUINEA-BISSAU		TUNISIA	
IVORY COAST		UGANDA	
KENYA		ZAIRE	
LESOTHO		ZAMBIA	
LIBERIA		ZIMBABWE	

Your mark goes here

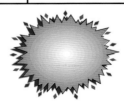

How Did You Do?

How did you go about remembering the capitals? If you are like 99.99% of the people on the planet you looked at the list, saw the capitals that you knew, like South Africa, and then started to bang the rest of the information into your head. Sort of like this, Algeria – Algiers, Algeria – Algiers, Algeria – Algiers, got that Angola – Luanda, Angola – Luanda, Angola – Luanda. Sound familiar? That is called rote learning and it is something that most of us stumble upon as we start learning.

The problem is that although we jam it into our heads we can't get the information out. Tell me if I am the only person that has studied for an exam only to discover that when I go to write it I can't remember a thing! Even shaking my head furiously did not get all the information out. I have got the information in my head, but it is all filed in the wrong place. It is the same way when we bump into someone that we have met before and then can't remember their name.

So how should we learn?

Have you ever watched children between the ages of 0 and 5? How do they learn? Well they have to touch everything, ask lots of questions, everything has to go in their mouths and toys must be thrown or at least dropped. That reminds me of a friend of mine that came home one day to find his kid with a live cockroach in his mouth. The child was just wondering what the cockroach tasted like. You see children have a very active imagination. That's why they will invite you to a tea party with 4 empty chairs around the table and insist that you greet Tom, Sally, George and Cindy. You see in their heads all of those people are really there.

The strange thing is that we look at kids and say that they will grow out of it. However children up to the age of 5 learn more during those 5 years than they do for the rest of their lives!

The human brain is programmed to learn using all 5 senses. However when we go to school we are told that black ink on white pages is just as much fun. This takes our learning from our childhood, which is 3 dimensional (using all 5 senses to experience height, width and depth), and makes our mind now learn in 2 dimensions (e.g. writing on a page).

Take a minute, close your eyes and think of somewhere you like to go e.g. the beach, a mall. Did you see it in colour, were the sounds crisp and clear, could you smell the sea air or the restaurants? You see we all store information in "movie clip" type pictures. That is why if you had to remember scenes from your favourite movies from years ago, you could. You've stored the "movie clip" in all 3 dimensions, particularly the scenes that made an impact like humorous scenes, action scenes or gory scenes.

That's why in this book we take you back to your happy places to show you how you can use what you already know and enjoy to learn easier, quicker and with greater recall!

Section 1
Preparing
To Learn

1
Physical

The success of any student can be greatly enhanced by getting some basics in place. Increasing competition for tertiary education positions has placed a higher level of stress to succeed on todays student. It stands to reason therefore that if our top level athletes are willing to change their diets, fitness plans, relaxation techniques, sleep patterns and increase the number of practice sessions just to improve their best times or their goal kicking ratios then we need to get our "Preparation Factors" in order if we are going to improve our learning success ratio.

In the following chapters we will look at the physical preparation, the mental preparation and the time management preparation basics that we should all have in place in order to enhance our learning capacity.

Body Exercise

Most people exercise with an aim to improve

muscle tone and function. However exercise also improves our hearts ability to pump oxygen-rich blood to every region of our body and as a result improves our health and cognitive function. Exercise also helps us to cope with stress, which is inevitable for any student. It also improves our mood, our mental health and our mental performance generally. It doesn't take a rocket scientist to work out that some form of regular exercise will have a huge impact on our mental performance. Exactly what you do is a matter of personal preference but studies show that the most effective exercises are those that get the heart rate moving, things like aerobics, swimming, running, brisk walking, canoeing and cycling. There are many more but the key is to choose an exercise routine that involves a sustained period of work.

Brain Exercise

If you were chosen to compete in the world body building champs in 6 months time, what is the first thing that you would do? You would probably drop this book and run to the nearest gym. How many of us would wait for the night before the competition before going to gym? If you did there are only so many arm curls you could do before the muscle would get tired and could not lift another weight. Even if you started curling those little weights that are used in aerobics you would still only be able to lift so many before the muscle turns to jelly and can't lift any more. Well our brain

is also a muscle! There is only so much information it can take before it can't take any more.

The good news for our brain is that it can be exercised in two ways. Firstly by body exercise which we have seen increases the bloods oxygen carrying capacity. This reaches the brain and in a similar way to muscle building, improves the quality and functioning of our brain. Similarly, by exercising the brain with some of the memory recall and speed reading techniques we will discuss later, we can increase its ability to think, hold and recall information. Like any exercise, the results will of course only appear with repeated practice!

Look at the chart and say the **COLOUR** not the word

YELLOW   BLUE   ORANGE
BLACK   RED   GREEN
PURPLE   YELLOW   RED
ORANGE   GREEN   BLACK
BLUE   RED   PURPLE
GREEN   BLUE   ORANGE

Left - Right Conflict
Your right brain tries to say the colour but your left brain insists on reading the word.

Breathing

There was an interesting study done on Tibetan Monks. They tested the amount of brain activity in Tibetan Monks and people that had just completed an intense aerobic workout. What they found was that both groups had the same level of brain activity. The strange thing was that the only thing that they had in common was breathing. Both groups spent a long period of time taking deep breaths.

The benefits of breathing are obvious, those who don't, die! But did you know that correct breathing can increase your energy, improve you health, increase your metabolism, help you sleep better and most importantly help you to think more clearly? So what's the secret? It's quite simple really. We need to breathe more deeply. As adults we tend to breathe from the top of our chests. This doesn't allow for a good flow of oxygen into our lungs and blood and as we saw earlier, oxygen-rich blood reaching our bodies and brains has many positive side effects.

A simple technique is to breathe in deeply for 2 counts, hold for 8 counts and then release the air for 4 counts, take 10 of these breaths. Do this 3 times a day and prepare to get dizzy because your body will get a huge surprise with the sudden inflow of oxygen!!!

If you continue with this exercise for a couple of days you are also likely to develop flu like symptoms. This is because as you breathe deeply there is more oxygen rushing through your veins and this clears out the toxins from your bloodstream and your body.

Healthy Eating Plan

Food and drink have the ability to improve our recall ability or to slow down our recall ability. That's why we often increase our caffeine intake around exam time in order to keep us more alert. Alcohol, on the other hand is generally avoided until after the exams as this has the opposite effect!

Unfortunately though sudden increases in stimulants at pressure times can have a detrimental effect on our concentration and recall ability. The "downer" from drinking 8 cups of coffee the night before a big exam may manifest itself during the exam and leave us wondering why we can't remember a single thing from the night before.

For maximum effect our eating and drinking should be regular and balanced. There are hundreds of books and diets on the market suggesting different ways to eat and drink and I'm not planning to add to those in this book. Most of us know what's good for us and what's not. We also have a pretty good idea of what a healthy eating plan is (even if we don't practice one!), so set yourself a regular balanced diet and stick to it, particularly during exam time!

Sleep

Dictionary Definition of Sleep

A condition of body and mind such as that which normally recurs for several hours every night, in which the nervous system is inactive, the eyes closed, the postural muscles relaxed and consciousness practically suspended.

As in all the physical factors before this one, the key here is consistency. Different people have different sleep needs and by this age in your life you should be pretty aware of how much sleep you need to perform at your optimum. The amazing thing is that in spite of knowing our optimum sleep period, students consistently adjust their sleep patterns during high pressure times. This is not to say you won't get away with it - adrenalin will usually see you through that big exam, but for optimum recall and concentration, regular sleep has no equal!

2
Mental Preparation

Music

"Give me control over he who shapes the music of a nation, and I care not who makes the laws"

Napoleon

Have you ever studied with music on and noticed that you start to sing the words to the songs or start humming to the tune? Well what this seems to suggest is that you are not fully concentrating on your studies but rather learning a new song!

So is listening to music bad when you are studying?

NO!!!

There is no doubt that music affects our mental state, our heartbeat, our emotions and our moods. Every known culture has music and it would seem that it is

---

one of the basic actions of mankind. Music is also an integral part of who we are, and as such it can assist us in learning.

There is much research on this subject, particularly in the area of Baroque Classical music. The popular opinion is that playing Baroque music will calm you down and greatly improve your ability to memorise information. The general consensus however is that it is not only Baroque but Classical music in general that has this ability. The reason is that this type of music is ordered and as such it releases neurons into the brain which help the body to relax and the mind to concentrate and perform more easily.

Astro.Trivia

The best choices for this exercise are Baroque Classical and Mozart as this music has a 60 beats per minute pattern which activates the left and right brain.

The key factor however is that you find classical pieces that you enjoy, listening to music that irritates you will hardly evoke the responses outlined above!

Do not compromise with rock, kwaito or pop music. Tests have proven time and time again that this type of music has a strong detrimental effect on the ability to absorb information into our memory banks. In fact, any music with lyrics should be avoided.

Ps. Don't let your mother read this page.

Your Study Spot

Where you study can and will affect the quality and quantity of the information entering your memory bank. A suitable study spot is essential. However, the word "suitable" can be very subjective in it's interpretation. Your parents and teachers would probably recommend a nice quiet place with no distractions, a hardback chair and an empty desk. To most students this sounds like prison and immediately removes the desire from them to even go and sit down, never mind actually learn something! Unfortunately the flipside of that coin is the student perspective of "suitable", which looks something like a towel on the beach or a bed in a room with loud music playing. Neither option is optimal for study purposes, but both have some points worth noting. Below is a graphical illustration of an optimum learning environment.

Study away from the TV or siblings who might distract you with noise or conversation	Avoid telephone interruptions; prime your family to take messages & yes your Cellphone does have an off switch.	Make sure your chair isn't too comfortable as this may send an incorrect signal to your brain i.e. it's time to sleep
Make sure you have all your stationery on hand - especially the creative stuff		Make sure you have access to all your study material before you start, this does not include food!!!
As per our section earlier, have some classical or Baroque music playing.		Study in the same place as often as possible. This programs your brain to think study when you go there, this does not apply to your bed.
During your break, don't watch TV 1. It puts your brain into neutral. 2. Even the most boring TV shows suddenly become very interesting	Have a watch or clock handy so that you keep your sessions to a set time. We recommend 20 minutes study, 5 minutes break	If you are 19, you've probably been on earth about 7500 days, by now your brain knows when you lie on a bed it's time to sleep and when you watch TV it's time to turn off

OPTIMUM LEARNING ENVIRONMENT

3

Understanding 3 Dimensional Learning

"Imagination is more important than knowledge"
Albert Einstein

Remember in the introduction we said that we have become 2 dimensional in our learning, while possessing 3 dimensional brains?

So how do we reverse the process and re-ignite our senses in the learning process? Well read on, but as you do this, bear in mind that we will be talking interchangeably about two things, firstly putting our notes into a 3 dimensional format, and secondly, putting the information into our heads

---

for recall. The two things are separate, yet connected during the process of taking this information from 2 dimensions into 3.

Let's examine some of the ways this can be done.

Experience

Wherever possible one should try to experience the concept you are learning about. If you have "been there and done it," as the popular saying goes, you are more likely to recall the what's and the where's of your experience. For example, I've just returned from Disneyworld in Florida so I've experienced it in 3 dimensions. If someone were to ask me about it I would be able to recall sights, sounds, smells and even some tastes! Someone who has only read about it would not have the same recall ability. Sure they could learn about it in a book, but their recall would largely be based on the method of learning they applied - probably ROTE (mechanical or habitual repetition) more than anything else. I would clearly have an advantage.

Unfortunately we cannot always experience the concepts we have to learn and that is where our imagination and senses come into play.

Colour

When summarising notes either by creative charting or cue carding, colour is a critical stimulant in the learning process. The more colours I use the more my sense of sight is stimulated, thereby making recall easier. If you are a habitual note taker then break your sections up into different colours, preferably the colour relative to the topic you are summarising, e.g. red for war, green for trees or if you have a vivid imagination pink for war and purple for trees!

Colour though, generally works better in conjunction with some of the other stimulants, particularly creativity and pictures.

Creativity

The more creative the better, both when making charts and when learning. Our imagination is the key to recall! The more creative we can be the better the chances for recalling information when we really need it. Remember in being creative; always attempt to relate your imagery with that which comes to your mind. There needs to be a link in your thinking when you create so that the link will automatically return when you are trying to recall in the pressured atmosphere of an exam.

Pictures

Pictures tie up with creativity as a recall stimulant. Even a simple picture in your **own** notes that links up with what you're learning will aid recall under pressure. Now you will have noticed that I highlighted **own** in the previous sentence and the reason for this is that it needs to be your own picture. Our textbooks often have pictures in them but if we "own" the picture by recreating it in our own notes and in our own way, the imagery will be stronger and the recall ability heightened.

In some sections it may even be possible to draw all the points in picture form!

Symbols

Symbols are another popular way of condensing long words or sections. Once again, the key to using symbols is that they are unique to you and easy for you to recall. Examples of more common symbols are:

< - smaller than
> - greater than
= - equal to
$ - dollar (or money in general?)
@ - at

rEMEMBER tHE mORE oUTRAGEOUS, cREATIVE aND cOLOURFUL, tHE eASIER tHE rECALL wILL bE

4

Time Management

Year Planners

One of the most difficult areas to deal with when faced with a mountain of paperwork, information from various sources, class schedules, social commitments and the need to actually pass at the end of the term, year or semester is "collation of data". The ability to put everything together in a logical format allowing us not only an overall view of where we are, but also allowing us to see where we're going. This is usually a very personal thing, some of us like diaries, some of us plunder on using crisis management and some of us use year planners. We, without a doubt endorse the use of "year planners" as the most effective way to manage your studies, revision, socials and exams, particularly in light of the mountain of information you will be bombarded with at Tertiary Level.

Where do I start?

Get a year planner. Either a normal paper one or if you can, a whiteboard type planner which can be used over and over again.

And then?

- Get all your tutorial letters, assignment dates (if they aren't in the tutorial letters), exam dates and times, holiday dates, public holiday dates and any other date that has significance in your life (sporting events, valentines day etc)

- Systematically go through each and every piece of literature you have been given and record all significant dates on your year planner. Use a pencil and cross out pages that have no significance either before or after removing the vital information. Use a different colour pen or highlighter for each individual subject or section if a subject is made up of two distinct topics. Be specific with all your entries.

- Record all your class times and venues.

- Now that you have recorded all your assignment due dates, mark out a day (a few days before each assignment) when you plan to submit your assignment or task, so that it arrives on time.

- Look at your exam dates and mark out the day that you will begin final preparation for each exam.

- At this stage your year planner should look quite daunting. It's now that you have the pleasure of looking for gaps where you could possibly take a short break or go away for the weekend.

And then what?

● Stick it up in a prominent place and refer to it daily! It holds the key to your success during the academic year.

Peaks and Valleys

Knowing Yourself

Another key to successful study is knowing your personal energy peaks and valleys. It would be a bit pointless to plan to study your most difficult section of work when you were in a semi-conscious part of your day. Far too often we study the easy stuff when we're most fresh and keep the difficult stuff for last, when we are too exhausted to really take it in.

Take the time to plot your daily peaks and valleys.

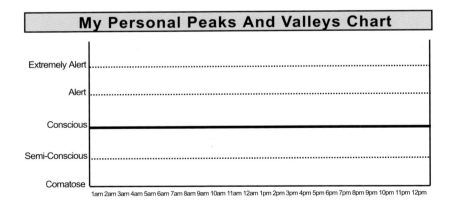

My Personal Peaks And Valleys Chart

Extremely Alert
Alert
Conscious
Semi-Conscious
Comatose

1am 2am 3am 4am 5am 6am 7am 8am 9am 10am 11am 12am 1pm 2pm 3pm 4pm 5pm 6pm 7pm 8pm 9pm 10pm 11pm 12pm

When and What to Learn

If you look at the chart on the previous page, you will get a rough idea of your personal energy peaks and valleys.

In order to study at an optimal level you should select the most difficult sections of your work and study these during your "Extremely Alert" and "Alert" times. Subjects you consider boring should also be aimed at these times. Work that you find easy should be aimed at any other "Alert" or "Conscious" time periods. It stands to reason that we should avoid studying anything during "Semi-Conscious" and "Comatose" times, however, there are studies that suggest playing tapes while asleep allows information to penetrate your subconscious!!!! Students who find themselves with limited or no "Extremely Alert" times should refer back to our section on **Physical Preparation.**

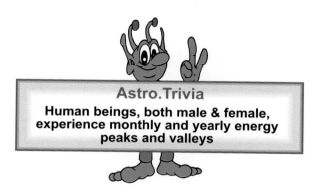

Astro.Trivia

Human beings, both male & female, experience monthly and yearly energy peaks and valleys

Section 2
Memory Techniques

Have you ever been with a group of friends and the subject of movies comes up? It's usually an interactive discussion as we generally all have a movie clip or two that we remember from some movie somewhere. Usually we remember the wild bits, the action scenes, the violent or the outrageously funny scenes. Rarely do we remember the five minute scene when the director slowly filmed the sun coming up!

Why is that?

It's simple really, the wild, funny, violent scenes leave a much deeper impact on our memory because they have a greater impact on our 3 dimensional learning area. Our imagination has been stimulated to such a degree that the scene is firmly locked into our memory and as a result easily recalled at any time. The key thing here is to take this same experience and use it in learning to take notes from the pages of our text books and place them in our memory so that we will similarly be able to recall them at any time.

There are several memory recall techniques in the marketplace today. You may already be using one or two of them and they may even be similar to the ones we will discuss here. I've chosen two, **Routes** and **Links**, as they are my favourite forms of memory recall and they work well. They also require the use of a very active imagination and all the senses.

Remember of course that as we practice these techniques it is important that you use your own imagination and pictures, colours and symbols that you understand. In memory recall it is always the link that is key and that's why it needs to be **your** link and **your** route and ultimately **your** imagination.

NB.

Essentially we will be creating "movie clips" for your brain which we will then use to recall the information at a later stage. You literally create a movie clip in your brain. The best way is to decide on your example and then close your eyes and see it happening. Include the sights, sounds, smells etc in your movie clip and then cut it, open your eyes and move on to your next clip. In the next section we will give you an opportunity to actually practice this technique.

5

Routes

The route method uses routes from our everyday life and attaches the information we are required to learn to points along that route. The kind of route I'm talking about could be something like your morning routine from waking up to getting into the car to leave, or perhaps the route you take when you go jogging. This method is best described by means of an example. If I had to remember a list of items that I needed to get at the supermarket, I would attach them to points along my "morning route."

Let's take the following ten items:
Newspaper
Milk
Washing Powder
Tuna Fish
6 Light Bulbs
Porridge
Soccer Ball
Box of Chocolate Biscuits
Shoe Polish
Toilet Paper

Now using the route method and my movie clips here is how I would remember the first three:

Point 1 – I'd wake up in a bed with a duvet made completely of newspaper.

Point 2 – I'd go to the toilet and after flushing, the bowl would end up full of milk!

Point 3 – I'd go to the kitchen, make a cup of coffee, which would froth up because someone replaced the sugar with washing powder!

This example is very simple and silly but it works and would even work with more complex examples. The key thing is to be creative and to keep it relevant to your routes. You will find that using this method will allow you to recall the information in any order, from the middle, forward or backward. The reason for this is that your route is so familiar to you that you can recall it in any order, as a result of attaching the items to that route; you will similarly be able to recall them in any random order.

Now you try using your morning route and create some wild, funny, creative movie clips. You have 5 Minutes starting ......

Write down the ten points from your memory

1	6
2	7
3	8
4	9
5	10

It is also possible to hold multiple sets of information. The more routes you have in your life, the more sets of info you can collect. The longer the lists, the longer the route you should choose. When I want to remember a list of fifty items, I usually use the route through my favourite supermarket!

BETTER MARKS in LESS TIME with MORE FUN

6

Links

We use the link method of recall when we are required to remember a word or phrase that links to another word or phrase. As in the route method, the key is to use your imagination and your links. We start by taking the key words and looking for familiar associations. We then LINK the associations and that is what helps us to recall the information at a later date. Let me give you an example. If I was required to remember all the 50 capitals of the countries in Africa I would do something like this:

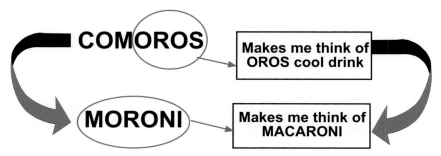

In order to link the capital of the COMOROS, MORONI, with the country I would create a movie clip of me eating macaroni, which is all in a bowl of OROS cool drink! Most of you will probably go "Ah disgusting man!", but that's the point. The image is so radical it will be easier to recall.

Now let's look at a slightly more difficult example.

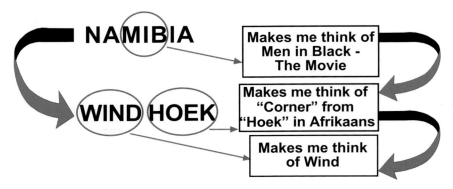

For Namibia I always see the mib which reminds me of MIB (the movie Men in Black) so I would link the capital to the country by creating a movie clip of Will Smith (star of the movie) coming around a corner (Hoek) with a strong wind (Wind) blowing in his face as he offloads his laser gun.

Now let's try a really difficult one.

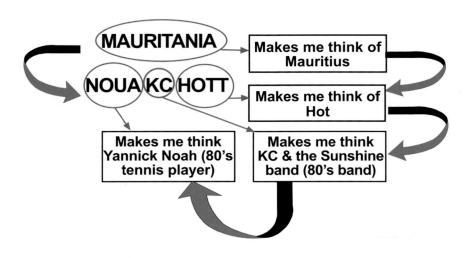

When I see Mauritania I always think of Mauritius. Nouakchott, the capital, is slightly more difficult to relate to as it does not create any immediate link. Like Windhoek in the previous example, I have to break up the word in order to get some potential words or images. So after breaking it up as indicated above and creating my links, it's time to create my movie clip. I'm on a beach in Mauritius watching KC & the Sunshine Band performing, it's early evening and it is hot, hot, hot! Everyone is in their swimming costumes and we are all having a good time. Suddenly the whole concert is disrupted when Yannick Noah's tennis ball hits the main system and it explodes.

Now you try one.

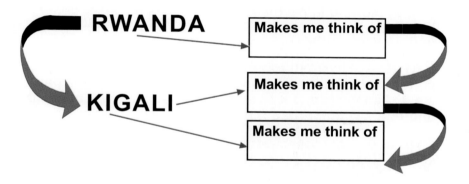

It's important to note that this method is relational and is best used for link type remembering only.

Routes and Links Together

I can also use a combination of the two methods when I'm faced with more difficult information or information that is not common to my everyday experience. Let's say I needed to remember the ten countries of South America listed below and I used my morning routine to bank them in my memory, it would go something like this:

Argentina	**Chile**	**Ecuador**	**Peru**	**Paraguay**	**Uruguay**
Brazil	**Suriname**	**Venezuela**	**Bolivia**	**Guvana**	**Colombia**

Point 1 – I wake up and see Diego Maradona jumping over my bed hitting a ball with his hand and scoring a goal, the crowd goes wild (Argentina)

Point 2 – I get up and go to the toilet where a carnival in typical Rio style is taking place, there is loud singing and dancing (Brazil)

Point 3 – In frustration I go and make myself a cup of coffee which burns my mouth in an unusual way when I sip it. As I scream out I notice that the cup is full of chillis and that's what burned me (Chile)

Point 4 – My toast jumps up out of the toaster and for some strange reason my surname is burnt into it? (Suriname)

And so I would go on. This may seem ridiculous but it really works. The weird associations are mine and I will recall them under pressure because they are my instant links. Maradona may not do it for you, but whenever I think of Argentina I think of him and that is the key - it must be your link. Notice also that in some cases the link is a person, in some event and in the case of Suriname it is what I think of when I see the word.

7

Sports, Hobbies & TV Shows

Another variation of the abovementioned methods is to use Sports, Hobbies & TV shows and just about anything else that is very familiar to you and your life. Here are some examples.

Sports

If I was a waiter at a coffee shop and I was required to remember all 15 types of coffee variations available I would use my favourite rugby team, The Natal Sharks, linking the 15 items to the 15 players I most associate with the numbers 1 to 15.

Here is an example

No	Item	Rugby Player	Link
1.	Cappuccino	Ollie Le Roux	I'd create a movie clip of Ollie running onto the rugby field wearing only a cap and a pair of chinos.
2.	Filter Coffee	John Smit	Filter makes me think of my pool filter so I would create a movie clip of John as my poolman cleaning out my sand filter.
3.	Dom Pedro	Deon Carstens	Dom Pedro makes me think of a Spanish man with a sombrero so I would create a clip of Deon propping down against an old Spanish guy.

Under pressure your brain will easily remember the 15 rugby players and then it's just a matter of remembering the movies clips, which, because they are 3 dimensional, will also be relatively easy for your brain to do.

Hobbies

You could use your favourite hobby to do exactly the same thing we did in the sports example. For example, if you enjoy chess then you could create links to all the chess pieces, both black and white. Be careful though that you don't use all the pawns as you may find the links getting jumbled in your brain! Here is an example using chess pieces to remember the names of some of our politicians.

No	Politician	Chess Piece	Link
1.	Nelson Mandela	Rook/Castle	I'd create a movie clip of Nelson Mandela sitting on the castle in Cape Town writing his book.
2.	Thabo Mbeki	Knight/Horse Rider	I would create a movie clip of Thabo Mbeki on a horse riding around parliament while giving a speech.
3.	FW De Klerk	Bishop	I'd create a movie clip of FW De Klerk dressed as a bishop and having a conversation with Desmond Tutu.

TV Shows

My favourite TV Show is "Frasier" and I could use that in the same way as the previous examples to link information to characters and thereby aid recall. Here is an example of how to remember the key tourist attractions in Egypt.

No	Egyptian Attraction	"Frasier" Character	Link
1.	The Pyramids	Frasier	I'd create a movie clip of Frasier polishing a set of specially designed pyramids, which he then places on his mantelpiece in a specific sequence.
2.	Cairo Museum	Niles	I'd create a movie clip of Niles in the museum interrupting the guide and asking a whole lot of ridiculous questions and upsetting the whole group.
3.	Camel Ride	Martin	I'd create a movie clip of Martin riding a camel and whacking it with his walking cane to make it move faster.

The examples that can be used are endless. The key is that you use those things that are familiar to you, your sports, your hobbies, your TV shows or movies. If it's relevant to you, you will find it easier to recall under pressure. If you've created a quality movie clip the recall of the required information will be relatively easy.

Section 3
Putting
It All
Together

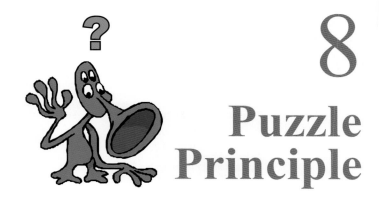

8

Puzzle Principle

Now let's look at how these memory techniques combined with our understanding of 3D actually applies to our everyday studies. We do this by starting with a process called the puzzle principle.

If you were going to build a puzzle, like most normal people, you would probably follow a certain chain of events.
1. You would look at the box cover to get an overview of what the whole picture looks like.
2. You would look at the specifications like number of pieces and puzzle size in order to determine how long it might take and what surface area you would need.
3. You would then proceed by removing all the straight edged pieces in order to create a border or framework within which to build!

Summarising Notes Follows the Same Principle

1. We scan the chapter to get an overview of what the chapter or section looks like.
2. We look for the "specs" like the number of main headings and subheadings in order to determine the size and complexity of the body of work we are planning to summarise.
3. We then proceed by transferring the headings and key points onto or into the chosen summary format.

The next page graphically illustrates the above principle.

How many main headings are there?
What does it mean?

MANAGING A SMALL BUSINESS

There are 4 main areas that have to be controlled and well managed to ensure that your business is successful. If you fail to monitor one of these areas the possibility of your business failing is great. What follows is a discussion of each of these 4 points.

1. Selling

This is an area that gets a lot of attention. However what does not get a lot of attention is customer relationships. This can greatly hook your existing customers to your business and prevent them from being stolen by your competitors. Another aspect of sales that is overlooked is selling the correct product. Most sales people make the mistake of selling anything they can to the client. This does not create a trusting relationship and can even stop the client from returning to your business.

2. Managing Finances

Most businesses fail because of not managing their money. You should always know what your product actually costs you. This includes production costs, transport, storage, advertising and rental. This will help you to ensure that you are charging the correct price for your product. Also you should always look to reduce your debt. Don't buy things that your company can't afford. Remember cash is king.

3. Staff

Failure to employ the correct staff will cause you to be fighting with people the whole day. A good staff member will attract the customers to come back. They will make your job easier because they will not need constant supervision. Always remember that you need to make sure that the person you employ is going to fit into the team.

4. Stock Control

Not taking the amount of stock on your shelves seriously will put a big strain on your finances. You should only have enough stock on your shelves to cover demand, with a few more as reserve. Do not have a reserve enough to cover the whole country in the event of world war 3!

Are there any diagrams or pictures?
What do they mean?
Why were they included?

How many sub-headings are there?
What do they mean?
What do they tell us about the article?

Is the material numerically structured?
Are there any bullets?

Other Questions

- *Is there a summary for the chapter?*
- *Is there a glossary?*
- *Do they highlight key words or points?*
- *Are there any shaded areas or information boxes?*
- *What is so important that this information has to be highlighted?*

BETTER MARKS in LESS TIME with MORE FUN

9

Creative 3D Charts

In the previous section on Summarising we used the Puzzle Principle to question, understand and extract information. The extracted information would then be transferred from the notes into a different format, which we call a "creative chart". This is not a totally new concept and most students should be fairly familiar with the process of maps or spider diagrams. As such our focus will be on the critical factors that relate to creative charts rather than how exactly you should do a chart. There is a simple example of a creative chart at the bottom of page 50 for those who have never done them before.

Key factors on Creative Charts to Aid Recall

- Use unlined paper and preferably A3 or larger. This allows for more creativity and imagination.
- Move your headings about; don't always place them in the centre or at the top.
- Don't get hooked on using words every time. Use colours, pictures and/or symbols where possible. If you must write, make sure it's colourful, bold and legible.

- Do creative charts while in class as you receive the information. It's a great way to take notes.
- Make sure it's personal. The more it relates to how you see it, the better the recall will be.

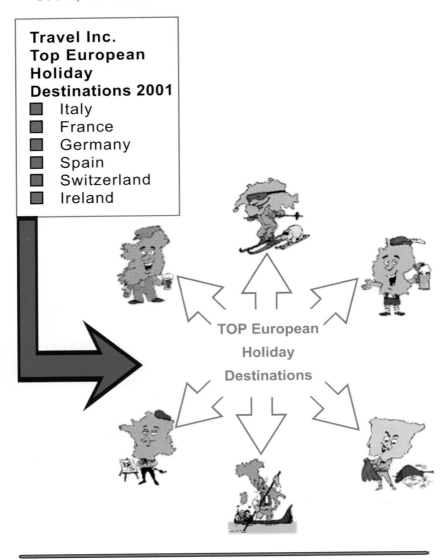

Travel Inc.
Top European Holiday Destinations 2001
- Italy
- France
- Germany
- Spain
- Switzerland
- Ireland

TOP European Holiday Destinations

Practical Example of a Creative Chart

U sing the article from the Puzzle Principle on page 48, this is how I would chart the information. Small Business Management (main heading) makes me think of a coffee shop. I would then use this theme through my whole chart. For Selling (sub heading 1) I see a waiter, for Managing Finances (sub heading 2) I see a till, for Staff (sub heading 3) I see someone serving at the counter and for Stock Control (sub heading 4) I see bacon and eggs!

The sub-points (i.e. information within the paragraph under each sub heading) will then run off of these.

Bad

Good

Section 4
Additional Study Techniques

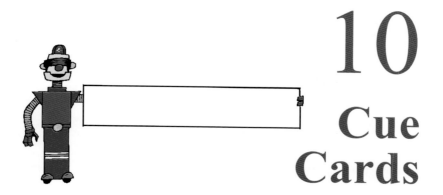

10

Cue Cards

Cue Cards are essentially small cards or pieces of paper that can be carried around in a wallet or pocket or stuck to everyday things. The most popular forms being carry cards and sticky cards.

Carry Cards

Carry cards are similar to playing cards and you can create your own set, almost like a pack of playing cards, with difficult formulas, points and definitions (remember to be creative). The idea is then of course for you to "carry" them around with you and have them handy so that you can pull them out anywhere, anytime and cover small sections of work. Think about it, in the queue at your favourite fast food outlet, while waiting for your mates at the beach, wherever and whenever you can get out your carry cards and in five minutes you could have a difficult formula or two committed to memory!!!

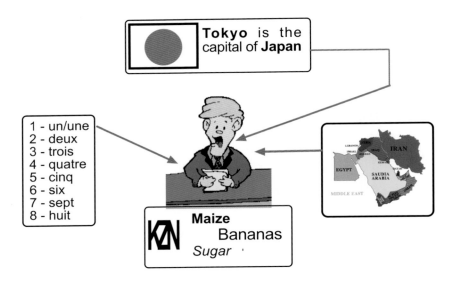

Sticky Cards

Sticky cards are cue cards with important information written on sticky paper and stuck around the house on things like the bathroom mirror, the fridge or the telephone. That way when you are doing those everyday things, like removing overnight fuzz off your teeth or gardening your hair, your memory is getting a work out!

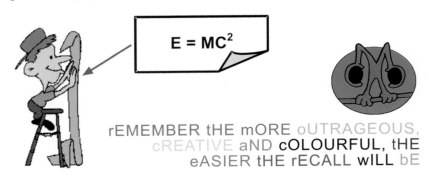

$$E = MC^2$$

rEMEMBER tHE mORE oUTRAGEOUS, cREATIVE aND cOLOURFUL, tHE eASIER tHE rECALL wILL bE

11
Mnemonics

Dictionary Definition of Mnemonic
.. a system designed to aid the art of improving memory

Mnemonics can be described as:

Rhymes or memory phrases:

- That generally use the first letter of words to create letters, verses or rhymes
- That help us to recall words, phrases, titles, facts etc.
- The most common forms being: Acronyms, Acronym Verses and Rhymes.

Acronyms

In its simplest form an acronym is a **made up word that is formed from the initials of other words** (e.g. NATO) and is pronounced as such.

Some other examples of this would be:

- USA   – United States of America
- UFO   – Unidentified Flying Object
- TRC   – Truth and Reconciliation Commission
- ROY G BIV   – Red, Orange, Yellow, Green, Blue, Indigo and Violet (colours of the rainbow).

Acronym Verses

Take the simple acronym a step further by creating short verses where the first letter of each word in the verse relates to the first letter of the word, phrase, fact etc. that you want to remember. In the above example of the colours of the rainbow we used a simple acronym, "ROY G BIV". That same example in an acronym verse would be: "**R**eally **O**dd **Y**aks **G**o **B**ananas **I**n **V**ereeniging".

Rhymes

Rhymes are a very old, but still very useful form of Mnemonics. Simply put, it is the process of putting facts into a short poem or rhyme to make recall easier. An example could be:

"The wind will blow from High to Low so Shakespeare wrote with his little toe".

rEMEMBER tHE mORE oUTRAGEOUS, cREATIVE aND cOLOURFUL, tHE eASIER tHE rECALL wILL bE

12
Study Groups

Study groups are a **powerful memory tool** in that they give us different perspectives on the same body of work.

Discussing the course with fellow students creates a memory recall tool similar to that of a personal experience. For example, earlier in the book, we discussed under experience that I would be able to remember a lot of where things were in Disney World, because I had actually been there, walked it out and lived the whole experience. If I had only learnt about it in a book, my recall of the facts would be more difficult. However, if I supplemented my reading of the book with **discussions** with people who had been there, and I then received their "**3D pictures**", my ability to recall the information would be enhanced. In the same way Study Groups add that "**discussion**" element, which ultimately adds to our memory recall ability.

Study groups are not social groups. It is important that you group with people who have the same study goals that you have.

Key Advantages of Study Groups

They allow us the opportunity to:

- discuss and debate sections of work
- share resources, experiences, notes, old exam papers and knowledge
- bring discipline into our study routine
- encourage others and be encouraged ourselves

Some Creative Ideas for Effective Study Groups

- Allocate sections for each member to prepare and present
- Organise a debate
- Brainstorm possible questions for exams (this is best done with the aid of past exam papers and assignments)
- Compare all the notes you have, particularly with regard to additional learning
- Have a quiz in the style of a popular TV quiz show

Section 5

Reading Quicker & Remembering More

13

Speed Reading

The higher the level you are in your learning life, the greater the amount you are required to read. At late high school or tertiary level particularly, we are required to do an inordinate amount of extra reading. With all the assignments, exams and very important social functions this becomes a very difficult thing to do. We're left with three options: either we don't do it, we sacrifice our social life completely or we learn to read faster!

What you need to do now is read the following article on the next page for 30 seconds.

Ready

Steady

Go, Go, Go!!!

The Water Bearer | 3

A Water Bearer in India had two large pots' hung on each end of a pole which	20
he carried across his neck. One of the pots had a crack in it; the other pot was	38
perfect. The good pot always delivered a full portion of water at the end of the	54
long walk from the stream to the master's house, but the cracked pot arrived	68
only half full.	71

For a full two years this went on daily with the bearer delivering only one and a	88
half pots of water to his master's house. Of course, the perfect pot was proud of	104
its accomplishments. But the cracked pot was ashamed of its own imperfection,	116
and miserable that it was able to accomplish only half of what it had been made	122
to do.	124

After two years of what it perceived to be bitter failure, it spoke to the Water	140
Bearer one day by the stream. "I am ashamed of myself and I want to apologise	156
to you."	158

"Why?" asked the bearer. "What are you ashamed of?" The pot explained why it	172
felt a failure. The Water Bearer felt sorry for the old cracked pot, and in his	188
compassion he said, "As we return to the master's house, I want you to notice	203
the beautiful flowers along the path." Indeed, as they went up the hill the old	218
cracked pot took notice of the sun warming the beautiful wild flowers on the side	233
of the path, and this cheered it up somewhat. The bearer said to the pot, "Did	249
you notice that there were only flowers on your side of the path, but not on the	266
other pot's side? That's because I have always known about your flaw, and I	280
took advantage of it. I planted flower seeds on your side of the path, and every	296
day you've watered them. For two years, I have been able to pick these	310
beautiful flowers to decorate my master's table. Without you being just the way	317
you are, he would not have this beauty to grace his house."	329

Each of us has his own unique flaw. We're all cracked pots. But if we allow it,	346
the Lord will use our flaws to grace His Father's table. In God's great economy,	361
nothing goes to waste. Don't be afraid of your flaws. Acknowledge them, and	374
you too, can be the cause of beauty. Know that in our weakness we can find our	391
strength. The happiest of people don't necessarily have the best of everything-	403
they just make the most of everything that comes their way.	414

Number of words read in 30 seconds

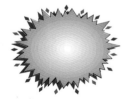

BETTER MARKS in LESS TIME with MORE FUN

The key to reading faster is simply this, do exactly the opposite of what your first grade teacher told you not to do – **USE YOUR FINGER!**

Our eyes are lazy and when we read they often re-read words we have just read. They also have a tendency to read the word above the word or below the word we are reading. This occurs more frequently when we are reading large portions of text. By using your finger you force the eye to keep up with the pace set by your finger. Ironically enough it is usually a pace the brain is quite comfortable with. In fact, with practice, you could improve your reading pace tenfold and the brain would keep up easily. Remember the brain is a muscle, which responds to exercise.

Another common question is, "If I read faster won't I forget what I have just read?" The answer to that question is no. Amazingly enough you will remember more. When you start to read faster, by using your finger, your mind starts to get excited. Your mind says "Yippee, at last some action!" It is because your mind is being challenged that it starts to pay attention and therefore it remembers more.

Let's put this into practice. We are now going to re-read the article using our finger to lead us. Your eyes should focus just behind your finger and you should see immediate results.

Number of words read in 30 seconds using your finger.

If this is the first time you have read like this, you would probably have been concentrating on your finger more than on what you were reading. This is ok because the more you practice this skill the less you will focus on your finger and the more you will retain the work you are reading about.

I practiced this reading method for 20 minutes a day for only 1 week and trebled my reading speed and doubled my retention.

The secret to this skill, as with all the skills presented in this book, is application! If you apply yourself and actually try the skills presented you will improve in those areas. Don't try once and give up because you don't get immediate results. Success always comes from hard work, luck is not a factor.

> **"The harder I practice, the luckier I get"**
> *-Gary Player*

What does the sign say?
Are you sure?

Section 6

Exams

14

Dealing With Anxiety

E xams! The very word conjures up images of hard work, no fun, hours of learning and anxiety. Life would be so much better if we never had to write exams, but hey, that's not going to happen so we best learn how to deal effectively with exams. We've already discussed in the earlier chapters how to learn effectively so that our learning time is reduced, this will already lead to reduced anxiety levels as we head into exam time. In order to further reduce exam anxiety we need to effectively prepare for exams and we will discuss those techniques in the chapters ahead. But first up let's look at some practical ways that we can reduce anxiety directly.

1. **Breathe Properly** – We've already discussed this in Chapter 1, where we said that breathing properly stimulates our brain functioning. Breathing properly and deeply can also stimulate our bodies, calm us down and reduce our levels of anxiety. When you're feeling stressed, breathe deeply and get your oxygen rich blood flowing.

2. **Relax Muscles Consciously** – If you are tense and feel a headache coming on, make a conscious effort

to relax all your muscles individually. Close your eyes and picture each part of your body relaxing or if you're really lucky get a family member or friend to give you a great shoulder or head massage. Be careful not to fall asleep though and miss valuable study time!!

3. **Go for a walk** – If you can, literally go for a walk. While walking make an effort to breathe fully and relax your individual muscles consciously. If you're in the exam room, go for a mental walk, close your eyes and go for a walk to your happy place. Be careful not to go on a hike, because this will reduce exam time and cause more stress!

4. **Think Positive Thoughts** – Your thought patterns can alter the state of your mind and body positively or negatively. If you are nervous about exams, because you think you are going to fail, this will manifest itself in your desire to study. The less you study will result in you being less prepared and more likely to achieve a bad result, which will in turn increase your stress levels.

Thoughts ⟶ Behaviour ⟶ Results

As you can see this is a self defeating cycle, which spirals downward. We need to arrest our thought patterns and reverse this cycle by changing our thoughts about life. Begin to think about all your achievements and the successes you've had. This in turn will manifest in your behaviour and attitude toward study, which will ultimately lead to better results.

5. **Visualisation** – Visualise your exam and the exam room. Picture yourself prepared and relaxed going to the exam room. See yourself answering all your questions, writing long essays and getting great marks.

This technique links to the previous technique in that it will enhance your positive thought patterns and ultimately reflect in your study behaviour. It's not only Olympic sportsmen that can take advantage of successful visualisation.

6. **Set realistic goals** – If you generally get between 50 – 60% then don't set a goal to get 90% (although the application of the techniques in this book could actually get you to attain that result), but if you don't get 90% this could demoralise you and affect further study. Rather set a goal of 65% and work towards gradual improvement. This will lead to regular short-term successes, which will endorse your positive thought patterns.

7. **Rationalise your feelings** – If you find yourself continually looking at a worst case scenario if you were to fail, and find that this is causing you a high level of anxiety, then apply this technique. Ask yourself exactly what the consequences of failing would be. Would you be able to rewrite? Could you do the year again? Would it really be the end of the world, as you know it? If you answer all these questions rationally you will realise that failure is merely a part of life.

15

Preparation Time

My worst exam nightmare occurred in the year that I wrote 2nd year Economics. There were two papers Macro and Micro Economics. They were coded ECN 201-A and ECN 202-B, similar but certainly not the same. When I wrote my finals I was convinced that I had passed Micro easily and that Macro was a close call. So when the results arrived and advised me that I had passed ECN 202-B and would have to write a supplementary exam for ECN 201-A in January I wasn't even surprised. I then spent my whole Christmas holidays studying Macro Economics furiously and arrived at the exam in early January ready to get at least a B. Imagine my surprise when I picked up the exam paper and found nothing that even resembled what I had spent a month learning! After the initial panic, stress and fear had subsided, I realised I had learnt for the wrong exam and as a result would have to do the whole year again!!

The lesson is obvious, "thorough" preparation is the way to exam success.

The 7 'P's of Preparation Prior to any Exam

1. **Practical** issues first. Make sure you know the exact date, time, venue and exam you will be writing.
2. **Prepare** an exam timetable which allocates revision for 3-6 weeks before an exam. Have a clear, concise plan of learning, which you block out daily as you achieve the prescribed goals. Allocate days for problems, which may arise, that need extra work.
3. **Plan** to get consistent sleep and consistent meals throughout your revision period (refer to Chapter 1) for optimum physical performance.
4. Mine **Past** papers, assignments and tests in order to gain an understanding of the types of questions that may be asked, the manner in which they probably will be asked and possibly find some that will be asked again.
5. Search study guides and work books for **Pointers**, particularly in the introductions and summaries that will direct you to the most important key words and topics that are likely to be covered in an exam.
6. Create **Possible** exam questions from your mining, research and study. Create an exam paper similar in structure to a previous paper.
7. Do the above-mentioned exam **Paper** under exam conditions in order to gauge your readiness for the exam. This paper should be done a few days before the exam allowing you enough time to revisit areas of concern highlighted by the mock exam.

16

The Last 24 Hours

Crunch time, and suddenly it's the night before the exam. Life becomes a series of decisions: Do I stay up late or get up early for final revision; do I get a good nights sleep or do I just study through the night; do I laugh or do I cry?

Writing exams generally doesn't rank on our top 10 list of exciting things to do on a weekday, but they aren't going to go away so it's best that we do as many things that make the experience less stressful.

We've already discussed in the previous chapter some key things that need to be done prior to an exam. The night before should therefore really just be a time of reviewing our creative charts and getting our thoughts and exam equipment in order. Lastly plan your course of action for exam day making sure that you have enough time to complete your morning routine and still arrive on time at the exam venue.

The Morning of Your Exam

1. Shower or bath to wake up thoroughly – dress comfortably and smartly, its part of the physiological preparation: look good = feel good = do good.

2. Have a good breakfast and something healthy to drink. It's really silly to have your body under pressure from lack of food while your brain is already under exam pressure.

3. Be on time at the exam venue. The stress of being late is something we can easily avoid.

4. If you need to go over notes, stick to reviewing what you've done or know. Trying to get into a new section will only cause panic.

5. At the exam venue avoid talking to people who are discussing questions etc. This generally just causes panic and can confuse you at a vital point in the process.

17

The Actual Exam

"The first and most important step toward success is the feeling that we can succeed."

Nelson Boswell

The 10 Point Check List

1. Make sure you have the right exam paper.

2. Read through the paper completely. Sometimes the multiple choice questions can help an essay question or vice versa. It's good to know this early!

3. Read the instructions on each question. Essays often have a choice of 2 of 4 options.

4. Allocate times and importance. Build in time at the end for contingencies, particularly if you are doing really well on one particular question and you go over your time allocation.

5. Write down your creative chart themes, mnemonics etc. Redraw them briefly if necessary.

6. Start with easy questions first to build confidence and get points in the bank!!

7. Underline or highlight key words in the questions so that you keep focused on what the question is about.

8. Leave space to come back to questions later.

9. Use the full time allocated to you for the exam.

10. Check that your answers correspond with exam question numbers before you hand your paper back.

18

Answering
Multiple
Choice Questions

When I was younger life was so much simpler in so many ways. The most significant decision I had to make was in the choice of chocolates. We had limited choices in those days and buying chocolate was easy. Nowadays however I'm confronted with at least 50 choices of chocolate every time I visit my local store!! Decisions, decisions! Why can't life have fewer choices?

In a lot of ways multiple-choice questions are very similar. It used to be that you had 3 choices, it was either a, b or c. Nowadays it's more like a and c, or a and b, or b and c, or none of the above, or All of the above or ..... The options are endless!!

Unfortunately there is no easy way to deal with the multitude of choices, but there are some ways we can make the choice easier.

- Underline the key words and circle the key requirement in the question. E.g. Which of the following are (not) countries in Africa?

- Try to answer the question in your head before looking at the answers as choices often confuse us. In the example above this would be impossible as it is based on choices. In that case go to the next step, which is to look at the answers and remove what you know is incorrect and tick what you know is correct.

- Check the answer requirement, is it a + b, or b + c + d.

- Answer the question but check the instructions to see whether a tick, cross or coloured in block is required.

- If your answers don't correlate to an answer option, go with your first instinct.

- If they are not employing a negative marking system, in other words, subtracting a mark for incorrect answers, then make sure you at least guess the answer!!

Finally, if you do need to change an answer, check the instructions on the exact procedure to be followed. It would be a terrible waste to have a question disqualified for something as simple as not following simple instructions.

19

Answering
Short
Questions

The key to answering short questions well is identifying the key words. Here is a list of key words and how you would set out answering the question.

Analyse   Divide into smaller units and then discuss these in detail.

Compare Differences   Either identify what is the same or what is different between the facts, or examine what the differences are between the ideas, facts, viewpoints, etc.

Contrast or set-off   Highlight the differences between the points or characteristics.

Criticise   Show the good and bad characteristics. Then give your own opinion once you have looked at all the facts.

Define or give the definition	Give a short and concise description of the subject or topic.
Describe	In a logical and well-structured manner, name the characteristics of an object or topic.
Discuss	Discuss a topic by examining its various aspects. A critical approach should be followed.
Distinguish	Highlight the differences that distinguish between two objects or topics.
Evaluate	Give your own point of view or opinion about a topic. Remember to measure them against the standards listed.
Examine	Critically discuss a topic in terms of defined criteria or guidelines.
Explain	Explain and clarify the points to make sure that the reader clearly understands you. Do this by making use of illustrations, descriptions or simple explanations.
Give	Give only the facts. Discussion is not needed.
Give an outline	Present the information in a brief, logical and structured manner.
Identify	Give the most important points or characteristics of a topic.
Illustrate	You can give clear examples or even draw a picture to get your point across.
Interpret	Give the meaning of the aspects in terms of a well known concept so as to make your explanations more practical.

List	Give a list of the information requested. Remember to do so in a specific order.
Name	Give the points, names, characteristics, items or facts.
Offer comments	Give your own personal opinion.
Point out	Give an accurate and logical account using sound reasoning.
Summarise	Give the most important points of a topic.

- Always answer the question that you know the best or the questions that you find the easiest. Not only will this give you a good confidence boost, but you will most likely get the most marks for these questions.

- If there are questions that you do not know too well, still try to write something. Just write down all the facts that you do know. Don't try to fool the marker by writing long answers, as they won't be fooled. Stick to the point and remember every point scores a mark!

- If you are running out of time, still tackle your best questions first and then tackle the rest. Remember, just write down the facts that you do know, don't waffle.

Important
Use simple English!

- If you have extra time at the end of the exam, go through your questions and change any obvious mistakes. If you are not sure if you have made a mistake or not, leave it.

BETTER MARKS in LESS TIME with MORE FUN

20

Answering True & False Questions

The true test of intelligence is not how much you know, it is what you do when you don't know!

Anon

True and false questions are generally a less popular form of exam questioning and invariably, when included in an exam, not worth much percentage wise. As a result thereof we should not spend a long period of time deliberating over true and false questions if we're not sure of the answers.

Here are a couple of simple rules when answering true and false questions.

T   F   1   Underline key words and circle key requirements in the questions

e.g. South Africa is (not) on the Southern tip of Africa

T F 2 Look for key requirement words like <u>all</u> (circle) or <u>never</u> (circle) as these make blanket statements about facts and unless <u>all</u> (circle) refers to "every single solitary one" the answer is false

T F 3 If any part of the question is false, the answer is false.

T F 4 Unless negative marking exists, guess!

T F 5 People in glass houses should throw stones.

If you haven't answered true on the first four questions above, best you check your answers now!

21

Answering Essay Questions

1. Read the question to see exactly what they are asking for. Look for and circle the key words.

2. Start by doing a quick planning outline.

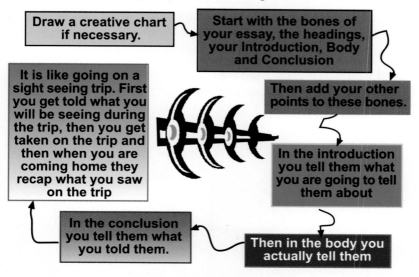

Draw a creative chart if necessary.

Start with the bones of your essay, the headings, your Introduction, Body and Conclusion

It is like going on a sight seeing trip. First you get told what you will be seeing during the trip, then you get taken on the trip and then when you are coming home they recap what you saw on the trip

Then add your other points to these bones.

In the introduction you tell them what you are going to tell them about

In the conclusion you tell them what you told them.

Then in the body you actually tell them

3. Don't repeat the question in your introduction. Rather take a stand in terms of where you are taking the essay.

4. Each paragraph should deal with a different concept and remember to always give your best points first.

5. Keep your sentences and paragraphs short.

6. Don't use words that are so big and grand that even you are not sure of what they mean.

7. Avoid slang, exaggeration and contractions.

8. Keep the tone formal; don't try to be the marker's big mate.

9. Don't generalise or assume knowledge of the marker.

10. Don't use quotations unless they directly support a point and if you do, always acknowledge your source.

11. Write neatly, the person marking also gets bored by your 2D offering.

12. Don't waffle to try and write a long essay in the hope of impressing the lecturer/teacher. This will probably have the reverse effect. Remember that they have many exams to mark. Make their job easier.

13. If you have time, re-read for errors as we tend to write fast under pressure and don't make sense.

Bibliography

Music:
- www.baroquemusic.org
- www.innerpeacemusic.com
- www.howtolearn

Learning:
- www.petech.ac.za/sc/lecture%20material.htm
- www.csbsju.edu
- www.dushkin.com
- http://nsml.nsm.iup.edu

Speed Reading:
- www.ucc.vt.edu
- www.mindtools.com
- www.trudeau.com

O'Brien.D (1993) How to Develop a Perfect Memory. London, London

D'Adams. DR P (1998) The Eat Right Diet. Century Books Limited London

Tape Set. Mega Speed Reading – Howard Stephen Berg

www.mindtools.com/pages/article/new ISS_03.htm
www.frll.com/~geomanda/mnemonics.htm
www.wm.edu/OSA/dostud/moresski/memory.htm
www.sleepfoundation.org
www.coun.uvic.ca/learn/program/hndouts/studygr.html
www.vic.edu/depts/counselctr/ace/stalygroup.htm

Jordaan, W.J & Jordaan J.J (1992)

Man in Context 2nd Edition, Isando, Lexicon Publishers (Pty) LTD

Robbins, A. (1986) Unlimited Power. London, Simon & Schuster

Mathews, M. (1990) Learn How to Learn. Cape Town, Don Nelson

van Schoor, W.A. Effective Study – Guidelines for Students. UNISA